CONFESSIONS
Of an
UNREPENTANT RHYMESTER

By

Wilhelmine Estabrook

Order this book online at www.trafford.com
or email orders@trafford.com

Most Trafford titles are also available at major online book retailers.

© Copyright 2009 Wilhelmine Estabrook.

All rights reserved. No part of this publication may be reproduced, stored in a retrieval system, or transmitted, in any form or by any means, electronic, mechanical, photocopying, recording, or otherwise, without the written prior permission of the author.

Note for Librarians: A cataloguing record for this book is available from Library and Archives Canada at www.collectionscanada.ca/amicus/index-e.html

Printed in Victoria, BC, Canada.

ISBN: 978-1-4269-0997-9 (soft)
ISBN: 978-1-4269-0999-3 (ebook)

We at Trafford believe that it is the responsibility of us all, as both individuals and corporations, to make choices that are environmentally and socially sound. You, in turn, are supporting this responsible conduct each time you purchase a Trafford book, or make use of our publishing services. To find out how you are helping, please visit www.trafford.com/responsiblepublishing.html

Our mission is to efficiently provide the world's finest, most comprehensive book publishing service, enabling every author to experience success. To find out how to publish your book, your way, and have it available worldwide, visit us online at www.trafford.com

Trafford rev. 5/15/2009

 www.trafford.com

North America & international
toll-free: 1 888 232 4444 (USA & Canada)
phone: 250 383 6864 ♦ fax: 250 383 6804 ♦ email: info@trafford.com

The United Kingdom & Europe
phone: +44 (0)1865 487 395 ♦ local rate: 0845 230 9601
facsimile: +44 (0)1865 481 507 ♦ email: info.uk@trafford.com

10 9 8 7 6 5 4 3 2 1

DEDICATED
to
Robert F. Nielsen
With
Love and gratitude

FOREWORD

Growing up in the country in the far off time before television, we made our own entertainment, singing songs, telling stories, reciting poetry. At "sings" and house parties and dances, talented piano, guitar, accordion, banjo players and fiddlers provided the music. Then there were the well-known hymns and choruses we learned from the cradle. Since the Baptist and Pentecostal Churches had a strong presence in our community where consumption of alcohol is frowned upon, sandwiches, cake and tea were served during the evening.

Coming home in winter in a covered in sled drawn by a horse, my father would sing to the beat of the horse's hooves.

In the one-room school I attended to Grade 7, we were lucky to have the late Ola Everett as our teacher. On Fridays, after making us promise to finish our work and sit quietly, she rewarded us by reciting many of the lilting old poems like The Deacon's Masterpiece and The Highway Man. I was hooked on rhyme for life.

Later when I moved to Toronto I lived in a rooming house, along with writers, actors, jazz players, folk singers, painters and others. Like me, most had day jobs, but we all yearned to "be somebody." Wine, beer, conversation, jokes, songs, monologues, and poems and limericks were shared, while blues, jazz and classical music played in the background. I have a clear memory of sitting on a window seat in a house at the corner of Dowling and King, watching the sun rise over Lake Ontario, and listing to "Summertime" from Porgy & Bess, as the first street car rattled up to the stop. It was a heady time for all of us.

While supporting my writing habit, I worked in several dreary office jobs, where I sometimes entertained myself, making up ribald couplets about our bosses. I enjoyed the howls of laughter from my coworkers, until one of them inadvertently left a page of my work in the copier, for one of the bosses to find. He was not amused.

These poems are for all seasons and all ages. Some are light and smiling. Some may bring tears. A few don't rhyme, but most of them rock. I hope you find some you enjoy.

Wilhelmine Estabrook 2009

INDEX

Title	Page
I Like Words	7
A Red Satin Box	8
Freezing Rain	9
Spring in Carleton County	10
Where I'm From	11
A Pause in Spring Cleaning	12
A Smiling Day	14
I Want to Write	15
The Colors of Angels	16
Arbor Day	18
BC Logging	19
Summer Saturday	20
Barking Mad	21
Beware	22
Holiday Attitudes	23
Company Coming	26
Dancing to Mozart	28
After the Ice Storm	29
Fall	30
Fear of Falling	31
Finger Exercises	33
For Gnu the Gnome Knells	35
Groundhog Day	36
Humbug	38
I Am	39
I Hope She Likes Roses	40
I Like a Man	41
In the Attic	42
Learning to Fly	43
Let R.B. Bennett Be	44
Magazine Covers	45
The Monk and the Mouse	46
Mothers Day	47
Ode to Nackawick	49

Title	Page
No Santa Claus	50
Ode to a Mosquito	52
Ode to a Mowing Machine	53
The Tamarack	54
Ode to an Apple	55
Season's Greetings	56
Skipjack	57
T.V. Rap	58
Temagami	62
Thanksgiving	63
The Ax Hangs Heavy	65
The Tale of the Army Worms	66
There She Is: Old	68
A Woman That I Knew	69
This, Too, Shall Pass	71
My Time	72
Waiting for the Doctor	73
Walking to the Mail Box	74
What Should I Worry About First?	75
Wild Flowers	76
When I Try to Meditate	77
Harvester Hanna	78
Youth	79
A Gust of Wind	80
Autumn's End	81
Baby Ghoul	82
Ballad of the Biscuits	83
Remembering Carla	85
Kitty Cat Rap	86
Counting Sheep	88
Did You Know?	89
Don't Measure Me	90
Flu Shots	91
Greetings From Us Moldy Oldies	92
Jonquils in Jodhpurs	93
Late March	94

Title	Page
The Lilac	96
Lily of the Valley	97
Little Red Meets Robin Riding	98
Lovin' My Laptop	99
Valentine to an Octogenarian	100
Minette	101
Multi-tasking	102
My Dog Jake	103
News From the Boonies	104
Old Woman on the Back Porch	105
Once I had	106
Once Upon a Sunday	107
Is This Sunshine	108
Spring	109
Susan Plays the Piano	111
The Misfit	112
Some Day You'll Be Middle-Aged	113
The Thief	114
Truly Tired	115
To Robert on Our Anniversary	116
Today's All That Matters	117
Summer Heat	119
We Need Trees	120
Valentine's Day	121
Sleepless in Wilmot	123
When Elephants Spin Taffeta	125
Write Time	127
Writer's lament	129
A Sky This Blue	130

I LIKE WORDS

I like words and what they say.
I could play with words all day.
Packed with letters, tall and short.
Weaving words is my chosen sport.

Zippy words, peppy words,
Words plum and pithy.
Archaic and moldy words,
Hoary words and mythic.

Words that preach and proselytize,
Explain, expose and emphasize.
Words that quiver in righteous rage,
Words that giggle down the page.

Commas make me shiver.
Hyphens make me moan.
Question marks are lovely.
On a dot they stand alone.

I long to scan and parse and phrase,
To ponder all the magic ways
That words can tattle, teach and talk,
Entice, enthrall, enamor, shock.

Limericks delight me.
Odes make me weep.
Soft-worded lullabies
Rock me to sleep.

I like words.

A RED SATIN BOX

A red satin chocolate box, shaped like a heart
I found in a drawer full of treasures.
It contained a pressed rose,
And some colorful prose
That brought memories of long ago pleasures.

Inside was a valentine, crumpled and worn.
It looked as if someone had bent it.
It said hugs and kisses
And words like forever.
Alas, I've forgotten who sent it.

FREEZING RAIN

What's that rapping at my shutters,
Flapping and rattling in drum beats and stutters,
Ticking and picking and clicking the glass,
Sticking, colliding and hiding the grass,
Glazing the gravel, sealing the soil,
Erasing all signs of the road workers toil?

The Chinook is over, the weather's turned mean,
The temperature's tumbling into the teens.
Wild winds and blusters, and cold freezing rain
Tapping and rapping at my window pane
Spitting and flitting and gritting my head.
Think I'll finish my coffee and go back to bed.

SPRING IN CARLETON COUNTY

When spigots placed in maples tall
Have sweet sap pouring from them all,
And chickadees on the garden wall
Send forth their lilting mating call.
You'll know it's Spring.

Hear bell-like trumpets sound below
The gritty, grimy, grizzled snow,
Of run-off in its yearly flow.
See crocuses put on their show.
At last, it's Spring.

When cattails spread in shaggy clumps,
By highways waved in thumps and humps,
From frost heaved pavement, full of lumps
The signs appear, slow down for bumps.
It must be Spring.

When grass turns green on every lawn
When St. John River ice is gone,
From forest edge come deer and fawn.
Days hold such promise with each dawn.
It's Spring.

WHERE I'M FROM

I'm from a few cells
Conjoined on a cold January night
By two tired people (homeless from a recent fire) seeking comfort,
Giving little thought to the resultant child,
Last of the litter,
Whose arrival nine months later would be as welcome as the bailiff.
I'm the breeched one,
Born feet first, head last,
Outraged at the injustice.
I came through long lines of
Celts, Druids, Danes, Normans, Saxons and Dutch,
From preachers and poachers,
farmers and philosophers,
Turncoats, tanners, tinkers and thieves.
I came from soldiers and cart wrights, blacksmiths and beggars,
Beer-swilling brawlers and barrel-chested men.
From clog-wearing, pipe-smoking, strong, whiskered women,
From women who stood by their men (and some who might have poisoned them).
From midwives and malcontents,
From bold adventurers and gay deceivers.
I came bearing genes from bakers, butchers and Irish trolls,
From merry-eyed kitchen maids and dowagers' gardeners.
I came from the earth which contained the bodies of the ancients,
Back to King David's water-bearer and beyond.
I came breathing air already breathed
By Alexander the Great, Joan of Arc and Jack the Ripper.
I came, listening to the spirits, talking to my familiar,
And other animals.
I came from long northern winters, out of mystery and peat smoke.
I came from seers and story tellers, from old women blessed (or cursed) with Second Sight.
These then are my ancestors.
I salute them all.

A PAUSE IN SPRING CLEANING

Gazing at faces in old photo albums
I've been communing with the dead
Clutching time-shrouded memories,
Departed friends, aunts, uncles,
Parents and grandparents,
Lovers, pets. All gone, long since.
Even the flowers are dead.
The buildings I photographed
On cold city Sunday mornings
Have been razed,
Replaced by high-rises or
Buried beneath super-highways.

Why do I grieve over prints on paper,
Torture my thoughts with pain and loss?
If those pictured were still alive
There would be little similarity
Between them and these photos,
These black and white faces on which
Much or nothing has been written.
Just tiny specks of stopped time.
Little girls now music teachers, grandmothers.
New babies, now fathers, soldiers, accountants.

I should take the albums into the garden,
Build a bonfire of twigs and sticks and paper
And toss them all in, one by one.
I should say goodbye to the parents and
Old neighbours. Forgotten friends.
I should proceed with my mourning
In ritual raving and moaning
Watching the flame and smoke cauterize
Memories rich and raw to scattered ash.
Then I could begin my life anew.

But no. No, not just now. I'm not ready yet.
I'm not ready to walk naked into my future
Without my pictured paper past.
I'm not ready to break the thread,
To step forward without these crumpled
Crutches. If I throw the photos out
I may forget who they were. Or worse,
I might not remember what I am.
No. Not ready yet.
For now I will merely close the pages,
Put the albums back in the box,
Push the box under my desk.
It doesn't take up much space--
Nowhere near as much as the dog
Sprawled at my feet,
Or the books crowding my shelves.
I am through with the dead for the moment.
I will put them away, wipe my eyes,
And prepare supper for the living.

A SMILING DAY

A smiling day, no pressing chores,
No special reason to stay in doors.
No snow to shovel, no steps to sweep,
No ice to watch, no holes to leap.
No mosquitoes or bees to hum
But lots of birds to chirp and drum.
No grass to mow. Too soon for flies.
Not a single cloud in the azure skies.

The woodpecker, robin, jay and thrush
Flit cheerfully from tree to bush.
Buds and leaves are bursting out,
I want to dance and sing and shout.
I've found a well-marked path to stroll,
To soothe my heart and rest my soul.
With new life brimming, there's much to see.
These are the wonder times for me.

I WANT TO WRITE

I've lain awake most half the night
Conjuring some words to write
But so far nothing's come to mind
No tales, no thoughts to spell or bind.

Along the road I walk and walk
And to myself I talk and talk.
There must be something swift and sage
That I can say to fill a page.

There must be at least a million words
Rapier swift and sharp as swords
Full of wisdom, shards of wit.
Yet, here I sit and sit and sit.

THE COLOURS OF ANGELS

What are the colours of angels?
What hues are their shimmering wings?
Are they silver and gold like castles of old?
Are they closer to paupers than kings?
Are there boy and girl types of angels?
What is a small angel worth?
Are all angels thin and do they have skin
Like the various peoples on earth?

Are they young or old or quite ageless?
Are they always happy and bright?
Do they hover around your shoulder
As they keep you safe through the night?
I think angels come in all sizes.
They are just how you need them to be.
What, you don't believe there are angels?
Why, there's one near the top of that tree!

Oh, I know that one's just an adornment.
Though it sparkles, it's merely a doll
With silken spun hair and glittering wand,
And she's only a few inches tall.
I truly believe there are angels because
So many times they've been there
When I needed the gift of a joyful lift
Out of the sloughs of despair.

My angel's been close through each illness.
It's brightened the gloomiest day.
It's taken my hand and it's led me
And readily shown me the way.
One once helped me avoid a collision
By guiding the wheel of my truck
When I lost my nerve on a wet icy curve.
(Oh, sure, you can call it plain luck.)

But I know my angel was present,
In the cab, right there by my side.
I sensed it. I heard it. I felt it.
And the glow of that presence abides.

I can't tell you the colour of angels,
But I've felt their wings brush my face.
I've heard their song as I've travelled along
And been filled with immeasurable grace.

An angel was called "a familiar"
By my grandma of Irish descent.
She was gray haired, had little round glasses
And always wore lilac for scent.
(Which is just how I pictured her angel.
Gentle. Encouraging. Fair.)
Yet mine's always close when I need it.
Like Macavity's cat, it's just there.

And I'm sure there is one special angel
On earth for each girl and each boy,
Sent down from above in the spirit of love
With a message, a promise of joy.
So, the tree angel is also a symbol
Of glory and hope and good cheer
Not only nearby at Christmas,
But all through the days of the year.

ARBOR DAY

Third Thursday in May.
Arbor Day, tree planting day. So
Plant a tree.
Plant a great tree.
Plant just one or two or three.

Plant a tree,
Just a small tree.
Any tree will be a tall tree
All that's needed is a seedling
And a shovel or a spade.

Plant a tree.
Plant a new tree
Plant a pine or beech or yew tree
Plant a cedar, oak or spruce tree.
Plant an aspen, ash or bass tree
Plant a willow for the shade.

Plant a tree
Plant a crab tree.
Plant a hickory or a walnut.
Plant a butternut or chestnut
Plant a hazelnut or beechnut
Plant a cheery cherry tree.
Plant a tree.

Plant a tree.
Plant a tree now.
Plant a tree and watch it grow.
See it changing with the seasons.
There are hundreds of good reasons
Why we all should plant a tree.

BC LOGGING

While the logging truck is being loaded
Gas drips on the ground. Hot oil fumes
Gush from the motor. A fire
Has abandoned the black stumps, stretching
Between the charred corpses of trees.

Diverted mountain streams strong with ore
Like bloody urine, gouge the roadside.
Whining tractor-trailers snake around
The rock-cut out onto the bay.
A whistle screams
Jarring the wilderness.

Above and beyond the glacier-fed streams,
The chain-saws have ravaged the trees,
Savaged the forest, leaving untidy gashes
Scabbing the mountain-side.
The once green and glossy
Growth of centuries-old Douglas firs
Have been torn away.
Gone for all time.

SUMMER SATURDAY

Eight o'clock Saturday morning
On the penultimate day of June.
Jake, the golden retriever, and I
Toured the premises, walked to the line fence.
It is a glorious morning,
Dawning clear and warm, a glorious
Summer morning,
full of import and opportunity, a new
Day in my life, a day full of promise,
Hope and expectancy.
A day like none other has ever been.
A day that will only come once. A day of adventure.
A day full of power and possibility.
A day to sing.
A day to pray.
A day to say,
"This is my life. I will live it with panache."
A day to say, "I love you."
A day to pay respects, to be gay and loving.
A Saturday, the day before Sunday.
It is a day for yard work,
A day to play with my silky silly dog,
To skip and trip on being alive.
Oh what a day! A clowning cat, popping out in purrs.
A marvellous, excellent, not bad, very good day.

BARKING MAD

What makes my dog bark endlessly
When there is nothing she can see
Except a squirrel or chickadee?
It really does annoy me.

Why can't she sit by silently
And leave the barking all to me?
Why must she growl and yap and yip
And wag her tail and curl her lip?

Why she does this is a puzzle.
I think I'd like to close her muzzle.
I'd glue it shut with peanut butter.
Then see what kind of "mrufk" she'd utter.

BEWARE

No vicious cut or savagery
Can match malicious piety
In pitiless brutality
To poison our society.

Beware those with ability
To recall each iniquity
Of lesser folk like you and me
To injure with cold treachery.

Undaunted by complexity
And blinded by pomposity,
Devoid of all humility,
Have they forgotten charity?

Deliver us from she and he
Who, scorched by pop theology,
Have erased true divinity
With a flame-throwing deity.

Dispatch with all alacrity,
Those butchers of tranquillity.
There's every possibility
They'll choke on their hypocrisy.

HOLIDAY ATTITUDES

Don't you love the holidays
The Christmas garlands, bells and sleighs?
The dinners, concerts, office parties?
The chocolates, liquorice and Smarties?
Don't you enjoy the wondrous sights
The shortbread, mincemeat, and the lights,
The cider and the ribbon candy?
The hand-knit socks will come in handy.
To bad it comes but once a year.
We could do with much more cheer.

Ho ho and bingle jells.
In my opinion Christmas smells
I just loath the festered season
As folks abandon sense and reason.
They trample you to death in stores.
They blare canned music out of doors.
Fat beggars on the busy streets
Annoy you for bucks and treats.
I hate ribbons, wrapping paper.
I despise this buy-hype caper,
The hostile shoppers, tired clerks.
And figgy pudding is for jerks.

I love it all, the candle glow,
The flickering lights and drifting snow.
I love the songs. Anticipating.
The cooking odours. Decorating.
I like the skating in the park.
And walking homeward in the dark.
I love the angels, elves and choirs,
The sound of church bells, marking hours.
I love to ponder Christmas lists
And look for all those special gifts.

*Who needs that useless junk and trash?
I don't want to spend my cash
On presents no one likes or wears.
I hate the whining, drooling stares
Of spoiled selfish greedy brats
In snowsuits, boots and stocking hats,
Howling for dolls and games and sleds.
They should be strangled in their beds.*

I love the groaning Christmas tables.
The mistletoe and timeless fables.
I love the wreaths and crimson holly,
The ivy and the Santas jolly.
I love to choose a Christmas card.
String outdoor lights around the yard.
I love the scene of nativity.
The bustle and creativity
That takes place this time of year
It fills my soul with warmth and cheer.

*I think Santa is a whuss.
And he's no doubt a surly cuss.
His nose is red and that's the sign,
He guzzles too much beer and wine.
There could be cooties in that beard.
And I submit ho-ho-ing's weird.
To stop a sleigh up on the roof
Is nuts--if you need further proof.
When climbing chimney's he could fall.
And he has high cholesterol.
I would hate to seem prophetic
But Santa's likely diabetic.*

I wish you weren't a spoil sport.
I know you're not the Yule Tide sort.
As many years as I remember.
You've hated Christmas in December.

*To me the whole month is a loss
A waste of time and coin on dross.
As avarice is celebrated.
I'd say the season's over-rated.*

Well, it's your option I suppose.
To feel the thorn but miss the rose.
Seems that's the way some folks are made.
T'will always rain on their parade.
But if you'd rather feel the gladness
New hope will overcome all sadness.
Enchantment happens from the start.
When you embrace a merry heart
Come share with me the season's cheer.
Your Christmas blues will disappear.
Don't sit there an look so tragic
Come, enjoy the Yuletide magic.
Let's loosen up, and have some fun.
A Merry Christmas, everyone.

COMPANY COMING

The garden's hoed. The grass is mowed.
The lawn is lush and green.
The apple trees and crabs have bloomed.
The grounds are neat and clean.

The eaves are painted, mailbox too.
The dog-house straw's been tended.
The old blue pick-up's washed and waxed.
The fenders have been mended.

The mats are shaken, floors are swept.
Mirrors and windows shine.
Sinks are scoured. The shower sparkles.
It glows, this house of mine.

There's cake and cookies in the jar
There's ginger ale and lime.
My work's caught up first time this week
And I have some free time.

I wish someone would come by today
To see us at our best.
Instead, folks will drop by, it seems,
When the whole place is a mess.

When I'm elbow deep in "Oven Off",
Burnt fish makes the kitchen reek.
When the cats' upset the flower pots,
And I'm having a bad hair week.

When I'm cleaning chickens, worming cats,
Or in bed nursing flu,
When I'm running late, or going out,
With half a million things to do.

That's when folks turn in my gate
And cruise on up my drive.
When I step out of the shower to answer the phone,
That's when folks arrive.

Quick! Hide! They're coming up the walk.
I must get out of sight.
Oh, good! It's sister, Bea... "Come in...
"You gave me such a fright."

DANCING TO MOZART

In my journal November 8, 2004, I wrote:
    Around 2:30 this morning I awoke and got up to see if there was anything in the fridge worth eating. Since the dusk-to-dawn light was glowing outside, I didn't bother turning on inside lights, which might have alerted the other denizens of the household. Instead I switched the CD player on low (oh, the joys of having a semi-deaf husband) and listened to Mozart as I pulled out salmon salad sandwiches left from yesterday's lunch. I poured a glass of milk and sat down at the kitchen table.
    This CD of Mozart's Five Violin Concertos is one of my all-time favorites and as I munched, bathed in that wonderful sound, I glanced out the back patio doors. A deer came out of the bushes, then another one—perhaps a mother and yearling. They pranced back and forth and nibbled at the lawn. They glanced up at me now and then, twitching their tails.
    Suddenly, as if they could hear the strains of Mozart, they began a slow dance, with graceful leaps, dives and swans. They seemed to be performing in slow motion. They cavorted for five minutes or so. Then as the music ended, they flipped their flags in farewell and faded back in the woods. I returned to bed feeling truly blessed.

AFTER THE ICE STORM

It's a sparkling morning
Sun-diamonds adorning
Each needle and twig
On the ice-laden branches.

The pine trees are stolid
Though they're frozen solid
To the snow drifts below
That imprison each bough.

As temperatures rise
The cerulean skies
Are reflected in ice drops
Which spin prism dances.

There is snapping and crackling,
A sound of bells pinging.
At the feeder small birds
Are pecking seeds now.

The twittering finches
Are flying just inches
From a waiting cat's whiskers
Behind patio doors.

The blue jays are screaming
While I sit here beaming
And waiting for Spring.
My gladdened heart soars.

FALL

Fall is cranberry jelly and chokecherry jam,
Horse radish and pickles and carrots to can,
It's rye grain and barley and grain fields of gold,
A fire in the kitchen when mornings are cold.

It's acres of buckwheat in patches of red,
A last flash of colour in a small flower bed.
Sweet maidens, the sunflowers, all in a row,
With bowed heads in bonnets, and faces aglow.

It's storm windows and banking and turnips to pick,
Crab apple preserves and a cinnamon stick,
It's dill seed and mustard, the aroma of clove,
With sealer jars boiling in pots on the stove.

It's the harvester's clatter, the groan of the plough,
Long months of cold weather to get ready for now.
There are pumpkins to gather and also the corn.
Boots, hats and mittens will have to be worn.

But when warm flannel blankets replace cotton sheets,
And fall's busy season at last is complete.
We'd be peaceful and quiet, all cosy and nice,
Except for the presence ...of seven field mice.

FEAR OF FALLING

The day is bleak and dark and cold.
I feel used up and rather old,
All trembling and tearful,
Stumbling and fearful,
Irritable and cranky.
I've chapped lips.
My nose drips.
I cannot find a hanky.

Yesterday I took a fall,
And hit the wall.
On this unexpected trip
I cracked my hip.
And since a door was in my way
I even bruised my vertebrae.

Did I say I bumped my head
And struck my wrist
With a nasty twist
That left my hand all black and red?
And that said..
(Sorry if I bore)
But there is more.

Oh groan and moan. I've got the blues
But my constant falling isn't news
As you'll soon read.
When I was six and stumbled
My uncle called me tumble weed.

Even as my knees buckled
I sort of chuckled
To recall
(Before the fall)
How I used to climb a tree
Because
Way up high, I could see

The very top of Mount Delight
Oh what a splendid sight
It was!

Maybe I tend to move too fast
Rushing, afraid my day won't last
Long enough to do my chores,
Put on my coat and get out doors,
Or have the time for me to take
A book while I am still awake
And glimpse a new and foreign place
Where there is lots of open space
And nothing on the ground below
To hook my unsuspecting toe.

FINGER EXERCISES

I have scarred my fingers, burned them, cut them.
In cupboards and car doors I've shut them,
Scraped them, nicked them, backward bent them,
Stabbed them, wrenched them, tried to vent them
And still they work, no need for rest.
Knobby, blunt and still the best.

I think of things that my fingers do,
Like hold a flag to wave at you.
I use them to glue, twist, tickle and touch,
To tat, taste, twiddle, tinker and such.

These fingers straighten, bend and curl.
Signal, beckon, point and twirl.
Hold a pencil, trim a crust.
Shoo the flies, and hide the dust.

They sooth, they tug, they pet the kittens,
They lift the latch and mend the mittens.
They clean the toilets, comb my hair,
They pin and sew and measure a square.

My fingers tweeze and dial and pull,
They warn me when the kettle's full.
They sense the cold, the feel of silk,
Of velvet, cats' fur, freezing milk.

They knead the flour, starch a blouse,
Wring the mop and milk the cows.
They make the beds, change the pillows,
Snap photos of new pussy willows.

They tie the dog and worm the cats,
Pick up the mail and nail the slats.
They open windows, shovel snow,
Shut the doors when it's five below.

I'll keep my fingers to sort the beans,
To darn, to knit, to match the seams.
To hold a hymn book, pick a flower.
I use them a hundred times an hour.

And when I have some time to spare,
I fold them, then I say a prayer,
And marvel as the blessing lingers.
I am so thankful for my fingers.

FOR GNU THE GNOME KNEELS

There once was a brave gnome called Lou
Who found a gnat's nest in his shoe
To a castle in Ghent
He rapidly went,
On the back of a gnarled old gnu.

At the castle, the knight was seen sitting
With a knave on a knoll, teaching knitting,
Wearing knickers of lace
And pink rouge on his face
Which the gnome on the gnu thought unfitting.

As he knocked on the gate with his knuckle
He attempted to stifle a chuckle.
But the knight turned about,
Flogged the gnome with a knout,
Then smackered the knave with his buckle.

The gnome, with teeth gnashing in pain,
Knelt near the numb knave in the lane,
Said, "I left the gnat's nest
Inside the knight's vest."
Then the gnome rode the gnu home again.

GROUNDHOG DAY

A groundhog with face furred and pointed,
Who awoke feeling limp and disjointed,
With a lurch did arise
To peer out at the skies
Then returned to his lair disappointed.

He'd carefully scanned hillock and meadow
Searched long but in vain for his shadow.
As wind ripples and rifts
Whipped snow into drifts
He burrowed back down in his bed-o.

Said his goodwife Marmota Monax
"Hold on, while I tell you the facts.
For months you've been snoring
I find that so boring
I could snip off your snout with an ax."

Said he, "Six more weeks of your grumbling,
Your kvetching, and whining and mumbling
Will scrape my nerves raw
As a saber toothed saw.
Now go stuff your head in a dumpling."

As she scratched at an itch with a thistle
She pondered his penchant to bristle.
"No need to get crabby
You silly old tabby.
Snore on if you must. Just don't whistle."

When spring came at last—as it will
And the sun warmed each hassock and rill
Mrs. Marmot came out
And wrinkled her snout
And then gazed all around with a thrill.

Said Herr Groundhog, "Well, what did you see?"
"Green grass and new leaves on the tree.
Come see the shadows
And the birds in the meadows."
"I will but, first, please pour some tea."

HUMBUG!

What's a humbug, Papa, please?
Why it's a shoofly with a wheeze.
It's a creepy-crawly, little pest,
A cricket in a chequered vest.

A humming bird without its wings.
A stylish centipede that sings.
It's like a beetle, green or fawn,
That one might find upon a lawn.

Papa, give me one more hug.
Maybe it's like a doodlebug.
A giant crawler from the moors.
A bookworm that snuffs and snores.

Is it something in the sky?
A sort of apple butterfly?
A humbug is a minty sweet
A candy in the Christmas treat.

A humbug's music on your tongue
A favourite of old and young.
There, you're all tucked in and snug.
Now, go to sleep, my ladybug.

I AM

I am
A mountain shrouded
In cove mist, shaking city dust
From my shoes. I am trout-fishing
From a streetcar window
In the crystal heat of the
Harbour.
I'm here, staring at the sun
Face down in a ditch.
I am the wind you feel through
The mirror. The cloud shadow.
Sometimes, I am the curse you
Mouth in ecstasy, the kiss of
Whetstone on scythe.
Sometimes I am a snail.
Others, a laughing pebble.
Today, I am
Fireworks in a beer glass.
I carry the earth in my hip pocket.

I HOPE SHE LIKES ROSES

Fluttering onto Toronto's Bloor Street
From Meccano toy buildings,
Come the celluloid swingers
Painted on eye-brows
Twitching like crazy commas.
The fashionable, fun people
Hurling themselves from
Stoplight to stoplight.
Bloor Street, where
Shifty-eyed street people price
Leather-skirted women,
With tattooed arms.
Where Hare-Krishna with the bad breath
Of chastity bump into your aura.

I am window shopping,
Strolling,
Hands in my empty pockets,
Well-being on my mind, when I see him.
Up the street he hurries, his tattered coat
Flying out behind, his merry face frosted
By a week's gray beard.
In one hand, he carries a paper wrapped bottle,
In the other a rose-bud bouquet.
Who is the lady who shares his wine and
His park bench?

I hope she likes roses.

I LIKE A MAN

I like a man who likes horses and dogs
And one not allergic to cats.
With warm hands and wit
And one that won't sit
Down to dinner, still wearing his hat.

My kind of man is an outdoors kind of man,
Who shovels the drive when it snows.
I'd go for a man
With a grin and a tan,
Who trims all the hairs off his nose.

The right type of man, need not be the man
Who's handsome and comely and tall.
If he's thick in the middle
Or can't play the fiddle
Why that doesn't matter at all.

There's one sort of man, who's the right sort of man
The one I keep hoping to see
He may not have money
But he's kind and he's funny
And best of all--he loves me.

IN THE ATTIC

In the attic
A corset with whalebone stays,
A wind-up gramophone, dusty Bluebird '78s,
And musty Saturday Evening Posts.
Quilt forms for spider webs spanning the rafters,
A commode, porcelain pitcher,
China basin with pink flowers and covered chamber pot.
A bundle of Christmas cards, a bolt of rayon,
Burned around the edges.
Coat hangers and crusty chair backs.
A hand-carved cradle, bleached Robin Hood flour bags.
A secretariat, with a package of pen nibs
Under the decades of dusty desertion where I sat,
Young and dreamful, writing letters to
Movie magazines and yearning to be
"Forever Amber,"
In the attic.

LEARNING TO FLY

How can you ever learn to fly
If you've never taken a fall?
How can you hope to reach the sky
If you don't leave the earth at all?

How can you hope to change the world
If you live in the status quo?
How will find your purpose in life?
How will you ever know?

How can you reach above the clouds
If you are sitting on the fence?
No one's ever had a vision
While mired in common sense.

How can you ever enjoy the sun,
If you've never known the rain.
How will you recognize happiness
If you've never felt the pain?

How can you take the stars in your hand,
How can you know that glow.
If you're not willing to take a chance,
To roll with the ebb and flow.

How will you know what it's like to fly
And scatter the clouds on the way?
To feel the spotlight, forget the stop lights.
And follow your star in your way.

LET R.B. BENNETT BE

We have had enough of federal waste.
Just look at our empty senate.
But the silliest plan devised to date
Is to dig up R.B. Bennett.

We know R.B. made his fortune here.
We won't say he was greedy.
He gave out $2s and $5s sometimes
To the jobless and the needy.

Some say he was a statesman.
A true New Brunswick son.
But when he lost the election
He backed out on everyone.

He sailed away to England.
Bought an estate green and vast,
In a lavish country mansion
He settled down at last.
He took his seat among the Lords
When parliament was in session.
While back home New Brunswickers
Weathered the Great Depression.

Interred in an English Church yard
With proper pomp and rite.
A sarcophagus marks R.B.'s grave,
A grand, imposing sight.

And, now they want to bring him back
To the province of his birth.
To re-inter his bones again
In Hopewell Cape black earth.
But R.B. died over 50 years ago.
His remains have turned to clay.
Since he chose to live in Blighty.
In Blighty let him stay.

MAGAZINE COVERS

Five ways to lose weight.
Six ways to change your mate.
Seven ways to get a date.
How to slim the hips you hate.
Eight new summer dishes,
Eat green and delicious.
Brittany's seen with Alouishous.
Loaves to go with little fishes.
Four ways to get a tan
Five ways to please your man
Six ways to keep him true.
A diet that will work for you.
George Clooney's fantasy.
Paris Hilton's ecstasy.
Doran Newton's chastity.
Star Wars' new entity.
Six creams that keep you young,
Seven treats touch your tongue,
What to wear, now spring has sprung.
New hope for cancerous lung.
Cheap ways to stay in fashion.
Eat well on low ration.
George Bush will face the nation.
No Iraqi occupation.
Cool clothes for moms-to-be.
Attitudes that set you free.
Baby new accessory.
Rooting out your family tree.
Counting ways to be and buy,
Counting things that you can try.
Counting, counting, wondering why,
Just spend it all before you die.

THE MONK AND THE MOUSE

There was a bad tempered monk up near Cleve,
Who found a cute little mouse up his sleeve.
He beat and he bashed
He waved and he thrashed
And trashed the whole house over one little mouse.
Now isn't that hard to believe?

The mouse didn't take up much room
It didn't burp loudly or boom
It was furry and soft, when it came from the loft
So, why did he go wild with the broom?

Said the mouse, as he ran down the road
I'm sorry I slept in your robe.
But it smelt like a nest, the kind I like best,
I thought it was a cape, and I had to escape
From a ferocious and big barking toad.

The monk he fell out of his tree.
"That sounds like a story to me.'
He said as he lunged,
Missed the branch and plunged
Into the lap of a small bumble bee.

"Now what have we here?' the bee said.
"A monk with a bump on his head?
"From whence did you come?
"Are you just acting dumb?
"Or, maybe, you're already dead?'

The monk shook his wattles and spoke,
"Though to you this appears as a joke.
If you give me the buzz,
I'm calling the fuzz,
I'd be gone, except the branch broke.

MOTHERS DAY

Happy Mothers Day. Have a carnation? No, thank you. I am not a mother. I am childless. I am barren. I may look like a mother, even a grandmother. It's an easy mistake, but I'm fallow, a fraud, a freak in the family of womanhood.

Never had any children? No. The only babies I have are those who haunt my dreams and die of my incompetence and neglect. And these are your children? How nice. How kind of you to share with me their graduation pictures. No. I have no photos of my children. How do you photograph the grey-veined blobs and liver of afterbirth? What shutter speed, what light density do you need to catch the pain etched on a soul?

Why no babies? Doctor said: an incompetent cervix...defective fetus...incompatible blood groups...mother's blood toxic to baby's...blue babies....ectopic pregnancy. (Oh, but I knew better. It was God's punishment. I was unworthy. I would have been a bad mother. I smoked. I drank. And so did the prospective father. But, nobody talked about that back then.)

No, I am not a mother. My last chance at motherhood ended in the spring of 1973 when my useless uterus was neatly excised, and hope died. No. I have not increased the population of an overpopulated world. I have never given birth to a rapist, a child molester, a lawyer or a politician, an autistic, retarded, encephalitic or addicted child, nor a murderer, a thief or a poet.

Still, time brings a kind of acceptance. My grief has progressed to the point where my sadness includes other women for whom Happy Mother's Day will always be a sick joke, a sharp reminder of the despair and longing that even decades do not dispel. I have come to understand the insensitivity of others who celebrate their biological wholeness, their ability to mate and multiply, to celebrate Happy Mother's Day. I can now look in a carry-cot and coo convincingly.

No. I am not a mother. I have never held a newborn in my arms, mine or anyone else's. But then I've never owned a hula hoop or solved the Rubik's Cube, yet I survived. I will survive barrenness, too. Perhaps I was an abortionist in another life. Or maybe in some former incarnation I smothered my children.

Happy Mothers Day.
No, thank you. I'm allergic to carnations.

ODE TO THE NACKAWIC PULP MILL

Oh, the country-side is luscious,
Trees in pale and emerald green,
Rolling hills and sparkling river,
Few more pleasing sights are seen.
There are cattle in the pastures,
Placid creatures moving slow,
Little suns of dandelions
In the fields just grow and glow.

Lilac, sumac, rose bush budding,
Apple trees and cedars spread.
Asters, pansies and nasturtiums,
Poking through the flower bed.
Surrounded by this floral wonder
How is it that I complain?
All the farmers will be happy,
'Cause it looks like we'll get rain.

When I came awake this morning
I ran to shut the window quick;
There a south wind gently wafted
With the pong of Nackawic.

Just an old pulp mill down river
Spewing sulphur foul and thick
It'd turn a hound dog off his breakfast.
Stronger than a pony's kick.
In comparison the barn smells
Seem as scented as the rose;
I could shovel there all morning
And not have to hold my nose.

I don't want to smell the pulp mill.
Would a protest do the trick?
I'd endorse most any action.
For I'm sick of Nackawic.

NO SANTA CLAUS

My father was a pragmatist, a realist.
He had no time for ghosts or spirits, or
Hustlers, hucksters or holy-rollers.
He couldn't be snowed with hocus-pocus.
Fortune-tellers got short shrift for him
(Though my grandfather read tea-leaves
With considerable accuracy, so I'm told.)
No lies. No artifice. No pretense.
He spoke the truth and expected truth
From his children. He also told us
That it cost nothing to be kind.
Father didn't celebrate Halloween
Or allow us to go trick-or-treating,
Said we didn't need to beg
Or make nuisances of ourselves.
Even without asking we knew
There was no Santa Claus.
One time I overheard him
Speak harshly to a relative
Who tried to scare my brother and me
With threats of the boogie man.
He taught us to respect our elders,
To stick up for the underdog.
To never back away from a bully.
My father taught us to face our fears
And my biggest fear was climbing.
One time he had me transfer a pulley
With coiled ropes from one eave of
A 60' high hip-roofed barn, to the other.
(Pulleys and ropes were used to haul
Hay-forks full of hay from the
Wagon to the haymows back then.)
With rope and pulley in hand I climbed
The ladder on the inside wall to
A platform two yards under the roof.
Balancing with one hand on a beam,
I blindly reached forward.

Cold perspiration leaked from my hands
and the soles of my feet, which were
teetering on the on the edge of the platform.

"Don't look down" my father cautioned.
"A bit further, you're almost there,
Further to the right, now to the left,
A little more. There. That's it."

The pulley caught over the iron hook.
My arms shook. My knees wobbled.
I clung like a limpet to the ladder
As I made my way to the barn floor.
Thus I conquered my worst fear,
Learned to face up to myself,
To listen calmly to the night noises,
To wait out the four-in-the-morning,
The suicide-hour panic and desolation.
I left the home place over 50 years ago,
But I could still find my way from
Cellar to attic with my eyes shut,
Or traverse the barn in the dark.
Father was right. It's still better
To confront the demons head on,
To consider the worst-case scenario.
Yet I'm neither brave nor courageous.
I no more take unnecessary chances.
I aim to stay off icy roads and climb
Nothing higher than a step stool.
And when my father, on his deathbed,
Saw and talked to his mother,
I did not interrupt.

ODE TO A MOSQUITO

The mosquito is a hateful thing.
It has a sharp and sudden sting.
It finds my bed when nights are hot
And searches for a tender spot
Beneath my arm, behind my ear.
It hums to warn me when it's near.
But, where exactly will it land?
Upon my nose on brow or hand?
It's hard to tell in dark of night
Just where that varmint plans to bite.
It dips and dives, soars incognito,
That pesky, wretched, lone mosquito.
I swat and slap the whole night long,
And listen to its battle song.
My nerves are shot, my eyes are red,
A throbbing pain beats in my head.
But then it leaves with stomach full,
And sheets down from my face, I pull.
At the last the torture is to end.
Oh, no! It must have called a friend.

ODE TO A MOWING MACHINE

When weeds of every height and hue
Reach skies of chicory blossom blue
When dandelion heads are showing
Or buttercups, it's time for mowing.

Though I prefer a natural scene,
To even cemetery green
I've wimped out to public trend
And crop my lawn from end to end.

Ignoring insects, noise and heat
I cut 'till every thing is neat
All sweaty when I'm done at last
I sigh, because it grows so fast.

Two days from now I'll start again
And if we get a lot of rain
The grass will then be twice as tall
You'd never know I've mowed at all.

THE TAMARACK

First to green out, last to shed, the tamarack
Blossoms in pearl-sized wooden roses.
A junk tree vying for fallow ground amid alders and pin-cherries,
The tamarack is not a fruit tree, not an ornamental,
Not a honey tree, not a resin or gum tree.
Not even very good for firewood is the tamarack.
Yet, when October winds have raped
The gaudy maples and last of the apples
Have rusted in the freezing sun,
The tamarack's burnished needles
Still glow a coppery flame.
Fall's final show before the snow.

ODE TO AN APPLE

Oh, there is nothing like an apple,
Red and juicy, crisp and sweet.
It's the best of any fruit
That you can buy or cook or eat.
You can core them, you can peel them.
You can tie them on a string
And then hang them in the attic
Where they'll keep until the spring.
You can chop them into mincemeat
Or in salad or in cake.
There's no end to apple dishes
You can slice or stew or bake.
There's apple jack, apple brandy,
Apple cider, apple sauce,
There's an apple for the teacher
And an apple for the boss.
There's apple butter, apple dumplings,
Apple pudding, apple pie.
Candied apples, glazed apples,
And the apple of my eye.
You can turn them into jelly,
Rich enough for any queen.
If you want to bob for apples,
You can do it Halloween.
But nothing's quite so nasty
To make one twist and squirm,
As, having eaten half an apple,
And then finding...half a worm.

SEASON'S GREETINGS

Already we're in mid-December.
I'm tapping brain cells to remember.
In vain I'm trying to recall
Amusing stories to enthrall
But, shrugging with chagrin, I find
The year's details have left my mind.

There were Sunday suppers, midday lunches.
Winds and rains and snow in bunches.
No travels we can brag about.
On Thursdays, took the garbage out.
The same day Robert went to Bridge,
I changed the beds and cleaned the fridge,
Swept fur and dust and washed the fleece.
Stayed ready for the house police—
(nurses, often without warning,
Would show up on a lazy morning
To catch my man and me both sleeping,
And cats, across the counters, creeping.)
We had some scares. We had some laughs.
I took a million photographs.
We rescued cats. We bathed the dog.
I walked in moonlight, wind and fog.
We played gin rummy, paid the bills.
Picked up prescriptions for his pills,
Inhalants, tubes and vaporizer.
I bought a bag of fertilizer
And planted two more rows of trees.
We snacked on grapes and wine and cheese.
We napped and read and worried some.
(Alas I ate when I felt glum
And packed on more unsightly fat
That can't be hidden by a hat.
And now to pay for all my sins,
I've developed three new chins.)
And, so, thus ends another year.
We send best wishes and good cheer.

SKIPJACK

All day the Skipjack skimmed the water,
The coast of Vancouver Island receding
Behind us, Japan out there somewhere.
Ropes and pulleys and fish-hooks squeaking
And clanging on the scaly deck.
It was a good catch.

The Skipjack is finished for the night,
Cradled in the roll of the swell, the fish
Are cleaned and packed on ice, the deck's been
Sluiced down to a faint odor of diesel fumes.

The singing kettle steams on the stove
While a lonely gull glides past the cabin window
Mirroring the late afternoon sun. The maps are
Rolled up and the stuttering radio is quiet at last.

I put away the supper dishes and enjoy the deep silence
While a tired skipper relaxes with his pipe.
Southwest winds breathe ocean air into the mountains
Now blue, now purple and then black
As the setting sun nods and blinks and departs
For the eastern horizon.

TELEVISION

Hail the TV! Teacher and master,
Peer of the realm,
Conductor, guru, boss, instructor,
Filling our hearts and minds with trash.
Raucous, ravenous, ceaseless monster
Creating a need, feeding our greed,
Styling and stealing our lives for cash.

Daily, hourly, countless faces
Flash across the screen.
A hundred thousand images
All vying to be seen.
Timpani and cacophony,
Prophesies and philosophies,
Theories and hypothesis;
Whatever does it mean?

All day the television's shrieking.
Wait, do I hear someone speaking?
What is it she is telling?
What is it he is selling?
Are they merely spelling
Words hypnotically?

Natural, herbal remedy.
Feel the cottony power
Energizing, amazing,
You will look younger
In only nine days.
Special offer. Guaranteed.

This news just breaking:
Floods, tremors, earth quaking;
Eight die in plane crash;
Oscars show up in the trash.
Trains derail, brakes fail,
Avalanche buries ski trail.

Shrinks haemorrhoids.
Academy Awards for
Best dressed,
Ultra new, ultra slim, ultra fresh,
Guaranteed to remove rust
Inspire lust,
Trust me.
No money down.
And no salesman will call.

Jack-hammer disasters
Endless pointless talk
Shrill demented laughter
Brittle as blackboard chalk.

Mass graves discovered,
More bodies uncovered,
Black box recovered.
Paul Barnardo's bid
For early parole denied.

Shoot, stab, eliminate,
Kick, punch, obliterate
See how we exterminate.

Thrill to the kill of road rage
You'll never have to turn a page.
The whole world's a small cage,
Inside our living room.

Weather warning
Global warming.
Students swarming.

New evidence of ethnic cleansing.
Deep down easy cleansing,
Get that fluffy, fleecy,
Just washed feeling,
Lemony soft.

See all the pretty people
Standing, talking,
Dancing, walking,
Swinging, swilling,
Swabbing, swirling,
Hustling, and muscling,
Pitching the latest product.

Buy this, get that,
No money down,
We're here to help you
Spend your life.

Blue skies, French fries
Hair dies, pork pies
Pecs, abs, tight thighs,
New cars, butter tarts,
Big trucks, body parts

Flaunting, flirting,
Pedalling passion
Showing all the latest fashion,
Faking caring and compassion.
If you're not buying
You're not living.
Amen, praise Jesus
Keep on giving.
You can reach us
At the address at the
Bottom of your screen.

Full-lipped, breasts bared.
In your face, sex blared.
Secrets shouted, tampons touted.
Civilization, culture, flouted.
All you never knew you wanted
Is yours for just
Three easy payments.
VISA and Master Card accepted.

The message is: you're worthless.
And, deep down, you know it's true.
You're ugly, smelly, spotty, hairy.
No one will ever want to marry,
The fat, unsightly--
Just floss nightly--
Lowly, loathsome loser: you.

Only body sculpted, anorexic
Like, totally, frenetic,
Super-smart jet-setter people
Really, richer, better people,
Are barfing caviar.
And that's a good thing.

You will be granted his approval
Just buy this instant hair removal
You'll be admired, loved, respected
You'll never ever be rejected
You'll never ever feel neglected.

Yes, you, too, can be adored,
Accepted, sought out, never bored.
What matters is the way you look.
You'll never have to read a book.
Don't think about the crack you took.

The promise is: the false is true.
You can be a brand new you.
With a new face, a new heart
A new life, and a new start.
Simply make that one decision.
They only make one small incision.
I saw it all on television.

TEMAGAMI

The June wind chants through the birches
White-capping the lake, while the boat
Rises and falls, caressing herself
Against the dock. Blueberry bushes scamper
Up the rocks to the cottage door.

Today the cottage is white and still.
And I talk to the trees and watch the
Nodding marigolds, yellow rows of tiny suns
Against the silent cedar horizon.

A sandpiper teases the bushes around the deck.
Quick she flashes, and she's gone.

My thoughts, usually a scattering of emotions
Is coloured joy and peace, and rest.
The changing seasons are time's attentive lovers
Of this northland, and
Knowing nothing is forever
Why does this day's end
Make me sad?

THANKSGIVING

One day when I was feeling dejected
Unheeded, un-needed and sorely neglected,
I heard a song running through my head.
It spoke to the moment. You know what it said?
"Count your blessings," the old hymn bid.
I took pen and paper and that's what I did.
I wrote page after page alphabetically
Day after day as things occurred to me.
Sometimes I remember things I have missed,
So I pull out that paper and add to my list.

There are animals, art, and abilities
Angels, aprons, and utilities.
Awakenings, aims and aspirations
Experiences, energy, expectations,
There're fingers, friends and family.
Flowers, freedom, and fantasy.
Boots, Band-Aids, beaches and bed,
Blossoms, a bicycle in the shed.
Coats, cats, computer, coffee,
Bath towels, blossoms, bread, toffee.

Chocolate, chowder, claret, choices,
Sunrise, daydreams, children's voices.
Duty, deer, delight and dishes,
Drama, doorsteps, chickpeas, wishes.
Hearing, eyesight, eggs, employment,
Feet, forgiveness, earth, enjoyment.
Fog, gaiety, galleries, grins,
Health, hope, hands, and safety pins.
Intuition, imagination, information sources,
Immune system, ideals, ice cubes, courses.

Juncos, jackets, jugs and jeans,
Juices, laces, magazines,
Mailbox, milk, mists, marigolds
Movies, muffins, moonlight strolls,

New shoes, clean clothes, no regrets
Good neighbours, good news, no more debts.
Oatmeal, oranges, and oil lamps,
Order, oven, pastas, plants.
Poetry, purpose, privacy, pines,
Patio doors, perfume and vines.

Silence, squirrels, rainbows, roses
Quilts, questions, dogs' cold noses.
Resilience, sunshine, round rocks, room.
Sewing machine, shower, scrabble, broom.
Shade, shirts, music, spinach, sky.
Sunbeams, stockings, and lemon pie.
Salads, salt, seeds, sage and seasons,
Why, there's a myriad of reasons
To give thanks for these and all the rest
And ever remember how I'm blessed.

THE AX HANGS HEAVY

"I'm old and cold and full of dread.
An ax hangs heavy above my head.
My husband, siblings, friends are gone.
And all I can do is linger on."
These are the words my mother said,
And sighed as she went back to bed.

Though I yearned to make a contribution
And gain, through duty, absolution,
I chafed and bristled with resistance,
And griped about my bleak existence,
When I should have been paying heed,
Relating to my mother's need.

And all those times we could have talked
But my resentful heart was locked
Behind the wall of callow youth.
I could not recognize the truth.
Her so-called golden age was dross,
Ruled by blindness, grief and loss.

But, did I pity, or recognize
My mother's pain, or empathize?
No, not in the years before she died.
Decades would pass before I tried
To understand her black despair.
But I do now. Because I'm there.

THE TALE OF THE ARMY WORMS

"They're back again," the neighbours called.
"You're bound to see them soon.
They've cleaned our ornamental bushes,
So, they should be there by noon."
I looked for some way I could stop them,
But it seemed our fate was sealed;
For lo! the army worms came marching, marching,
The army worms came marching
In a line across the field.

With my spray gun at the ready
I stood on guard beside the gate;
But even as I leaned there, waiting
I could see I was too late.
In the thousands they kept crawling.
Though I sprayed, they would not yield,
All those army worms came marching, marching,
Those army worms kept marching,
Up the middle of the field.

What a ruthless infestation!
Left me sombre and perplexed.
From the poplars they took breakfast,
And the cherry trees came next
Through the day and night they feasted.
Then the morning light revealed,
Those army worms now marching, marching
Those army worms now marching
From the middle of the field.

Not a plant left in the garden,
Leaves mere wisps of memory;
Brown and dead they left the forest
As far as human eye can see.
All the damage of their pillage;
T'will be years before it's healed.

After army worms went marching, marching,
The army worms went marching
Through the middle of the field.

Now I gaze out of my window
And see trees all bare and stark.
Not a green thing in existence.
Everywhere they've left their mark.
No more shimmering leaves on willows,
From the hot sun's rays to shield;
Since the army worms came marching, marching
Since the army worms came marching
Through the middle of the field.

THERE SHE IS: OLD

Yes, Old.
Untidy, leaky, noisy,
Cantankerous about the digestive system.
She's become one of those funny old ladies
She used to laugh at on the beach--except
She doesn't find it funny anymore.
She--one time, slim, svelte, clear of eye and skin,
Shining hair and regal carriage--has morphed into
She with the varicose-veined stick-legs,
The dowager's hump, the grey hair,
Wattles and liver spots,
The one who checks for pill box,
Depends, dentures, and trifocals,
Before she greets the day.
She wears sensible shoes,
Dresses for warmth.

A WOMAN THAT I KNEW

There was a woman that I knew
Who was very much like me, or you,
Who wanted all the best from life
To be a poet, mother, wife.
And, truth to tell, she did her best,
She never thought to stop and rest
Or take the time to feed her soul
While lying on a grassy knoll
With sunsets, or the scents of spring.
Up before the alarm could ring.
She always met her obligations,
Entertained the delegations,
Furthered her man's career,
Tried to take away the fear
Of failure, to be doubly sure,
With her support, he would endure.

Her house was always sparkling clean.
No dust moats, spider webs were seen.
She arrived at church on time.
Adorned the water glass with lime,
Seasoned beef for tenderness,
Added bits of watercress
To dress the salad plates, and eggs,
And rinse the coffee pot of dregs.

She should have sat and sipped some wine,
Soothed by Mozart, light, divine.
Driven, instead, she'd grab the broom
And sweep up crumbs in the dining room.
She wished she had more time to read
But she had a family to feed.
Floors to sweep, a budget plan,
The table to set before her man.

And she liked to dig bare toes in sand
Or stroll the park and hear the band
Play something like the Blue Skirt Waltz.
Or join the game of "True or False"

Her children played with shrieks of laughter
She planned to do all those things after,
To just kick back and have some fun.
Whenever all the work was done.
She always planned to visit more
With people she greeted at the store,
To stop and pass the time of day,
And hear the things they had to say.

But she was always in such a rush
To clean or iron, scrub or brush.
She always found a sink to scour
She used up hour after hour
Painting shelves or folding clothes
There was no time to smell the rose.
But always so much to be done,
No time to dream. No time for fun.
No time to wonder at it all.
To listen to the bluebird's call.

But now those folks are dead and gone,
And she is longing for the dawn.
Too blind to read, too deaf to hear
Haydn, Chopin, Mozart dear.
No longer does she wish or yearn
To sip some wine. The stomach burn
Would hurt so bad she'd almost scream.
The simple joys it would seem
She'd denied herself for much too long.
She's lost the lyrics of her life's song.
She seems so tired and so lame.
She hardly hears them call her name
To tell her that it's time for bed.
Somehow she feels already dead.

THIS, TOO, SHALL PASS

When I went out to retrieve the trash can, I decided to walk on up to the spring (or past the corner of my lot.)
It occurred to me, as I walked through the sunny morning, that the days we have to walk in air such as this are finite. A touch of melancholy came into my thoughts as I smelled the sweet hay, wild clover and whatever it is that smells like grape soda pop (the kind Sussex used to make). I noticed the grass and leaves dying back, the ravages of tent caterpillar, marsh grass and marigolds. It isn't just fall coming on, it is that I will soon be 68 years old, and am reminded that most of my life's allotment is now behind me.
I looked at the corner posts I painted a couple of years ago, and recalled tramping through the woods in high rubber boots, painting one slash after another and understood that there won't be many more years when I am physically able to do that.
I look at the flickering reflections of leaves in the breeze-rumpled brook and know there will come a time when I can neither see it, nor smell it, nor feel it, nor even walk by it.
We are here for such a little time.
It also came to me, while I stood waiting for some large high-wheeled (spraying?) machine to pass, how grateful I am to be living here in this exact spot, where people wave, where neighbors stop to chat, where the cats follow me, where the scent of apple drops teases my nose.

MY TIME

The computer's updated.
My cats are sedated
With catnip and liver.
So it's now or never,
I've earned the right
To write.

I've caught up the mail,
Both e- and snail.
I swiffered the floors
And wiped down the doors.
I've polished the mirrors.
They're clearer.

I've cleaned fridge and freezer.
Dehaired with a tweezer
My chin and moustache.
I took out the trash.
I viewed my profile
And smiled.

I've done all the dishes,
Disposed of suspicious
Containers and pots,
Of stuff I'd forgot.
The cats listen.
Whiskers glisten.

Ah, but today,
I must make my way
To the airport in Maine
Where soon once again
I'll meet my dear lover
Whose face I will smother
With warm puppy kisses.
What bliss, this!

WAITING FOR THE DOCTOR

Is it real, or have I imagined it?
Has this lump grown, has that mole changed?
Should I leave well-enough alone?
What if she tells me what I don't want to hear?
I know the word cancer, backwards and forwards
Inside and out. I have intimate knowledge
Watching people die with brain cancer
Bowel cancer and myeloma.
One decided against surgery, chemo and radiation.
Two opted for surgery. One is dead and the other dying
Slowly, painfully, angrily.
Another shot himself. (He was my age).
Whatever it is I've got I will not
Put my family through the hell
Of long dangerous winter trips
To the other end of the province
To wait with all the other brave,
Beaten, really, really sick people.
What will the results of my tests be?
More surgery? Has there been a recurrence?
Malignant or benign?
Has it gone into remission? Metastasized?
Is my body rotting from the inside out
Or the outside in?
When can I expect my brain to go?
Is my will in order?
Can I depend on my last wishes—
Cremation, no funeral, no memorial;
No coffin, no monument,
No grave? My ashes to be tossed
Into the cedar grove?
To whom should I bequeath my
Semi-precious stone collection,
The carvings, created by my beloved
Brother who died after a seventeen month
Battle with brain cancer and left me alone
With no childhood friend.
"The doctor will see you now."

WALKING TO THE MAIL BOX

Walking to the mailbox at the end of the lane
Wondering if the Christmas parcels
Mailed on the first of December 35 days ago
Will have made it through.
Or maybe there'll be a card,
Instructing us to pick them up at
The Post office in town.
I breathe deeply of the January air.
It's warmer than yesterday.
The odor from the horse stable
Across the road on the next farm
Mingles with spruce and pine,
And there is a tinge of wood smoke
Wafting up from the south--
All signs of another storm coming.
17000 times in my 69 years
I've walked to the mailbox.
And as many times my heart has
Beaten faster, drumming out
A frisson of anticipation.
What will it hold today?
A letter from an old lover,
A reminder from the insurance company
A photo of a friend,
A newspaper, magazine, flyer,
A statement of accounts,
A cheque from a publisher,
A notice from the hospital,
Scheduling surgery for cancer?
No. Today the mailbox contains
A late greeting card,
And a letter for my husband.
I flick down the flag and
Turn towards the house.
I notice that the days are already
Becoming longer, by the way
The sun filters through the pines.

WHAT SHOULD I WORRY ABOUT FIRST?

My friend's possible Alzheimer's
My sister's diabetes and anemia
My brother-in-law's multiple myeloma
My husband's emphysema
My brother's prostate cancer
Another sister's sore hand
The upcoming surgery on my nose?

Or the car accident in Centreville
A relative's schizophrenia
A neighbor's criminality
A daughter's precarious mental state
The unbalanced tumbler in the dryer
If the new pajamas shrunk
If I ordered the prescriptions
If I'm losing my short term memory
If I will write something today
If it matters to anybody
Whether I do or not
What I should make for dinner?

My list could go on.
Reach further afield:
Floods, tornados, wild fires
Children dying of starvation
Girls being molested
Women being abused
Men being tortured
Seniors being neglected
Hilary Clinton becoming president

But I guess I'll stop right here
Too much to think about,
Too confusing, too depressing
Too pointless to waste time
Worrying about wasting time.
Instead I'll go for a walk.

WILD FLOWERS

I counted the blossoms I saw today
As I meandered along my way
Through wood and rill, down vale, up hill
And by the pond, cool, clear and still.

I saw the apple trees in bloom,
And dandelions in their plume.
And roses where the bees could sup,
Marsh marigold and buttercup
I saw trilliums, lupines pink--
(One held the cheery bobolink.)
Strawberry petals small and white,
And violets open to the light.

There was adder tongue, aster, kale, and Wister's,
Dogwood, dogbane, Dutchman's britches,
Vervain, fleabane, plantain, rue.
Monk's hood and mustard, drenched in dew.
There were bluebells, blue flags, tulips, thistles
And teasels with their spiky bristles.
Chickweed, hawkweed, milkweed, cresses,
Primrose, daisies, ladies' tresses.

There was parsnip, wild, and Queen Ann's lace
And Lambs quarters about the place.
Loosestrife, lousewort, pokeweed, Phlox,
Goats beard, lavender, figwort, docks.
There was colts foot, fox glove, common mullion,
Caraway, garlic and wild onion.
There was dog tooth violets, ivy, vetch
And some whose names I couldn't fetch.

Paintbrush, beardtongue, morning glory.
Each blossom tells its own sweet story
On shore and field and park and lawn
In the summer in the Valley of St. John.

WHEN I TRY TO MEDITATE

When I try to meditate
I find it hard to concentrate
To free my mind and clear the slate
Or try my pulse to regulate.

I wish I could initiate
Opinions I could contemplate
Theorems that would germinate
Breakthroughs that illuminate.

But though I to wish cogitate
To ruminate and integrate
Before I can even speculate
My musings tend to terminate.

HARVESTER HANNA

She's a housewife and mother for most of the year
But she drags out her long-johns when autumn draws near.
With lunch bucket, thermos and cotton bandanna,
Into the fields rushes Harvester Hanna.

Harvester Hanna wears three pairs of socks.
She works on the potato belt picking out rocks.
Through dust, wind and sunshine, in spite of the racket
She soon starts to sweat in her warm winter jacket.

A lady of glamour, I'll confess she is not,
But without her the harvest would come to a stop.
So, she stays on the job 'till the frost settles in
And the potatoes not sold are all stored in the bin.

Please remember our Hanna when you next feast your eyes
On baked, boiled, mashed, or those golden French fries.
Our New Brunswick potatoes are enjoyed by all,
And she, too, plays her role in the harvest each fall.

YOUTH

I remember youth,
Trying it out, trying it on.
Experimenting, reaching ,striving, struggling,
Learning to be,
Wishing I was someone, something, somewhere else.
I remember anxiety, insecurity, passion,
Adrenalin charges that climaxed
In fear, exhilaration, pain
And tiny tendrils of hope.

A GUST OF WIND

A gust of wind
A dust of snow
Yet lust for living
Makes me throw

A woolen scarf
Around my collar
Put on a coat
And give a holler

To Pep, the pup,
Whose tail is waving
'Hurry up," says he
"I'm craving

"To get outdoors
And make my mark.
Your silly chores
Can wait 'til dark."

AUTUM'S END

The autumn's glory, all but lost.
October's pumpkins rot with frost.
The bitter winds that sear the bone,
That cause the naked trees to groan,
Will usher in November's moan,
And I, deep in melancholy, sigh and rave.
The leaves are gone, the garden's done.
Each day cheats with lesser sun.
There is no syrup, charm or pill,
No elixirs, strength of will,
To cure bleak old December's chill,
And dead white winter yawns like an open grave.

I light a candle, close the doors,
And, finished with my evening chores,
In easy chair I settle back
A purring cat upon my lap
And watch the evening sky turn black
As daylight fades from every ridge and nook.
And so my spirit inward turns
Where hope resides and longing burns.
I warm my thoughts with cups of tea
And count the different sides of me.
And dream of things that still might be,
Then turn for new adventure to my books.

BABY GHOUL

There once was a timorous ghoul
Who worked hard to frighten and fool.
But when he looked scary
The dog had a hairy
And tossed him into the pool.
So the ghoul went to Great Goblin School
And he studied the Halloween rule
In classes he'd loom
And he'd flap and he gloom
And he'd screech and he'd cackle and drool.
They dressed him in cobwebs and tatters
And covered his physog with spatters
He was gummy and sticky
And colored all yickky....
And gung-ho, and that's all that matters.
But when he ventured out Halloween night
In the harvest moon's cold yellow light.
There were monsters and tricksters
With broom sticks and whiskers
Which all made a horrible sight.
The ghoul wondered what he could do.
As a spook, he felt more like a stew.
He tried to look ghoulish
But only felt foolish....
And all he could do was "boo hoo."

BALLAD OF THE BISCUITS

Snow was falling. The wind had risen.
The day was dark and dirty.
Then sister Beatrice called and said
"Come up about 4:30.
I'm baking biscuits, warming pie,
And making hamburg stew."
"Why, thanks a lot," I said with joy.
"That's just what we will do."

I washed my face and creamed my hands,
And put on something festive.
We looked forward to an hour out.
My mate and I were restive.
We fed the dog, put out the cats,
Shut off the reading light.
We swept the steps and warmed the car,
The day turned dark as night.

The snow tires purred like kittens,
The main road was plowed bare.
I gave thanks for my mittens.
And drove along with care.
When we got to Beat and Aage's,
The snow was falling hard.
I whipped along the driveway,
Then did "wheelies" in the yard.

Beatrice was there to greet us,
And Princess dog was too.
We changed from boots to slippers,
And smelled that lovely stew.
Then in came Joe and Ursela,
And stamped off all the snow.
They hung up coats and parkas,
Their faces were aglow.

We all sat down to dinner,
And after Thanks was given.
I sipped hot stew and really thought
I'd died and gone to heaven.

Then Beatrice opened the oven,
And filling a baker's sheet
Were twenty-four fresh biscuits
All rowed up tall and neat.

The biscuit tops were golden brown.
The insides were creamy white
The texture soft as feather down.
I groaned in pure delight.
We slurped the stew with gusto.
We had some yarns to share.
The stew and biscuits vanished
Like dreams into thin air.

Then on came pie and ice cream
And squares and fresh hot tea.
When I couldn't hold another bite,
I turned and said to Bea.
"That hamburg stew sure hit the spot,
The pie and ice was fine.
The company was great as well
But the biscuits were divine."

REMEMBERING CARLA

Why, oh why, we plead and cry,
Do the young ones have to die
Before they've fully lived their time?
We see no reason, know no rhyme.
The truth that's often quite forgot:
One day we're here. The next we're not.

An act more futile, sad or lonely,
More painful than the words "If only,"
May be to pass the present in
The wasteland of "what might have been."
All we can count on is the "now,"
To do the best that we know how.

Yes, life is short, and then it ends.
We yearn and grieve for whilom friends,
But earth is ruled by a greater plan
Than any such devised by man.
Though the body rests beneath the sod
The soul, once freed, wings back to God.

KITTY CAT RAP

Twizzle, the kitten
Is forever sittin'
At my computer.
I try to scoot her.
When she's there, you see
It's hard for me
To read the monitor
So I gets onto 'er
Because I'm wantin' 'er
To move her butt.
She shrugs, as if to say: "So what,"
And kicks a flea in my direction.
"I cannot make the right selection,"
I scolded her.
She answered: "Purr."

Twizz weighs under 60 ounces
But I sure know it when she pounces on my mouse.
I grouse.
Even worser, there's my cursor
Disappearing off the screen.
That makes me mean.
Darndest cat
I've ever seen.
"Purr, purr."
Why, of why, oh why can't she
Let my old computer be,
Go climb a tree
Or chase the dog
Or roll a log
Or stretch out long upon the mat
Like any other pussy cat?

"You really have to move," I say.
"Find some other place to play."
Don't think I'm getting
Through to her.

She merely sits and answers:
"Purr."
I just want a game of Scrabble

But soon I commence in to babble:
"See what you made me do!
You made me waste a perfect "Q"
And, look, I even had the "U.""
But all my pleas mean nix to her.
She rumbles: "Purr."

"Get down right now."
I know she's heard,
She twitched her tail at every word,
Then yawned, "Meow,"
And stretched her back
And took a bow.
"Right now," I spat.
And then I smile
Just for a while
Forgetting that
I'm talking to
A doggone cat.

COUNTING SHEEP

Who was it said that counting sheep
Would put a weary soul to sleep?
I'm here to prove the man's a jerk
I've tried and found it doesn't work

I've added, numbered, toted, tallied
Some that came and some that dallied.
I've counted goats and bucks and does
And all their legs and tails and toes.

I've studied, as on them as I gazed,
While they sedately chewed and grazed.
I tried deep breathing, gaped a yawn
And prayed for rest before the dawn.

I've worked on kids and ewes and rams
And wooly lambs in their pajams
I've multiplied and guesstimated
Sets of triplets, I've cal'lated

And still you see I'm wide awake
What does it take (for pity's sake)
For this old dame to get some peace?
No baa-ing critter dressed in fleece

Has ever made me less forlorn
As I, wide-eyed, await the morn.
But come daylight, I'll rise and stretch
And wish a hex on that dumb wretch

Who stated that those blasted sheep
Would let old Morpheus creep
Into my aching, spinning head
To slumber sweet in my own bed.

DID YOU KNOW?

This morning the sun is dancing on the frosty window
Coloring the chimney smoke pink and shading
The winter lake with silver, while your soft memory
Lingers in the room.

Did you know last night when you were sleeping that
I touched your face, and you reached out to hold me?
Then I kissed your hand and held it, so
You wouldn't feel the tears.

Do you remember the first icicle you watched
Glistening in the sun?
The first spring robin?
Do you remember your first rainbow?
Fall maple?
Do you remember the first time you heard a nightingale?
Remember the awe and joy?
That is how I felt that first morning
When I opened my eyes and found
You lying beside me.

DON'T MEASURE ME

Don't measure me and my successes
By youth's criteria and excesses.
Allow me dignity and grace.
I've earned the right to wear this face.

I'm getting soft, and long in tooth.
I've lost the supple skin of youth.
My hair is thinner now, and grey.
I think I'll leave it, just that way.

Take what you see as what I am.
I won't be mutton dressed as lamb.
I see no cause to look or seem
Like thirty-five. I've made that scene.

Forty's gone and fifty, too.
So sixty should be something new.
New books, new insights, and new trends.
New foods, new flowers and new friends.

I'm not as swift as I used to be.
I'd rather admire than climb a tree.
I no longer scamper up the stairs.
I creak when I kneel to say my prayers.

But at life's rich banquet I plan to sup,
Of the wine of adventure I'll empty the cup.
If age dismays you, it's not my fault.
So, diet be damned, now pass the salt.

FLU SHOTS

We continue to be hebetudinous
With symptoms of flu multitudinous.
I've threatened to bludgeon
My darling curmudgeon,
If he says one more word, platitudinous.

His physog is damp and lugubrious;
His sneezing erupts like Vesuvius.
While I'm lachrymose
I lie comatose
And ponder the fate of the two of us.

He has coughed for what seems like eternity.
I've sweated and wheezed. Oh woe is me!
No potion or pill
Has cured us of this ill,
This truly tiresome infirmity.

So intent on some means of distraction
To survive this long trial of inaction
I rhyme words in lumps
In bunches and clumps,
So I won't have to put him in traction.

GREETINGS FROM US MOLDY OLDIES

We wish you lots of Christmas cheer,
A joyful season and New Year.
Our news is nil. Our lives are sweet.
We nap, we read, we rest our feet.
We watch old movies, or we talk,
Play Mozart, Chopin, Haydn, Bach,
Compete in Scrabble, Gin and Bridge,
He sips some rum. I raid the fridge.
We check the mail. We surf the "net."
How much better can it get?
We're grateful that we have so much.
That's all from here. Please keep in touch.

JONQUILS IN JODPHURS

It was a peculiar day in a strange placebo. It was the sneezing season, when wheezing walrus thronged and thrummed through the spaghetti fields, where Manx cats were hiding. Later I found their cattails in the swamp.
As I looked over the raisin bushes I noticed snapdragons and dog-tooth violets were sniping at a brace of toothless beagles gumming bunchberries.
It was a weirdest morning! Runner-beans were doing pushups. Although there wasn't mushroom, macaronis were flexing their elbows. Sugar Pops were trimming their corns and smoking corn-cobs while the corn huskies sang the blues.
The world stood on its end at a still stand while king fat cat Tupper II, sat on the scanner and saved four pink paw prints for the internet. Sight-challenged archers, eating arrowroot biscuits, practiced hitting bull's eyes, and jersey (clad) cows were leading blind bulls. Evening primroses were in mourning as the morning glories climbed the lattice- or was it lettuce-I can never remember.
Meanwhile the lambs' quarters all grew to fifty cent pieces. Marigolds made brass knuckles. Then it turned so cold pullets put on their pullovers. Katydids, pickled in porridge, did imitations of daffodils wafting aloft in the Febreze. Rosie ratted on the other katydid, who did what she was not supposed to do; she filled the giraffe's galoshes with crazy glue and dew.
But all was not lust. The bleeding hearts, wearing lady slippers and Queen Anne's lace, got transfusions as the queen and her entourage possied over the Firth of Forth. Yet card-carrying computers kept cumin in via the caraway.
You'd have laughed to see the hideous horde. The tooth fairy was so old he wore dentures and a duffle coat. Sundogs who'd watched too much of the Larry King show sported red suspenders and watched crocodiles dialed cellular phones while waiting in line at K-mart for bean crocks. Sadly the snowdrops came down with Hogwarts as jonquils in jodhpurs jousted with jolly Roget's.
At lunch time the cook, Captain Cook, A.K.A. Ralphie Crook, substituted a buttercup for 250 ml. oleo and fried a mellow yellow melon, marinated with mullion. Jacks got to thinking

outside their boxes of crackerjacks. Foxes lurched around with bare paws, since their foxgloves were stolen by treacherous Thatcher's catchers' mitt snatchers. Then the sky turned to milk of amnesias. There were no longer any sugar canes, only walkers--walking trees, actually, not to be confused with allegedly genetically-altered alligators.

You may think I'm making this up, but I swear I saw sobbing robins and weeping hyenas hiccoughing delicately in silkworm hankies. The blue-cheese moon beamed around the square pink and puce sky, as Tupperware clouds frothed and fluffed, and fumed at frost flakes filling window glass with diamonds. Turkeys were sucking their thumbs, after eating bear claws at Tim's. Cloned cormorants waltzed with unctuous uncles. Then the stars came out--Paris, Lindsay, Brittany and Brad--and helped themselves to gigabits of purple pabulum made of green peas in ipods. Talk about gulling the silly.

Anyhow, I could see there was more to this than meets the eye-liner. The willows dropped their pussies and, though it was only January, March hares were already hawking dust bunnies. I waited until the turtle doves grew taco shells and began cooing in Spanish. And that reminded me, to get supper started.

Hope y'all have a rice evening.

LATE MARCH

Can this be Spring?
I rather doubt. I had to get my woolies out,
A scarf to cover up my snout
To which the cat hairs cling.

Is this the last?
The steps are slick and thick with snow.
The temperature is five below
And more is falling fast.

When will it end?
I have a brand new shovel handle. It's a dandy.
Glad there're neighbors living handy.
There's nothing they can't mend.

It's not the worst
Weather-wise. The skies are bound to clear
And winter will be gone this year.
Tomorrow is the first.

First day of Spring
Why gripe and grumble or to mumble.
Watch your feet so you don't stumble.
Tomorrow robins sing.

THE LILAC

Purple, lavender and mauve
The lilac buds in May.
By June each lissome branch
Labors under cones of bloom,
Matchless bouquets
Of scent and colours.

The century old lilac bush at the home place
Has weathered four hundred seasons
Or maybe more.
Small animals scratch the earth at its root.
Birds nest among its branches,
Safely hidden,
Tending their nestlings.
Honey bees scout the bush for nectar.

The lilac bush has been clipped,
Cut back, pulled up,
Run over
And transplanted.
In June its blossoms fill vases,
Grace tables,
Pleasing nose and eye.

The lilac's purple party dress will
last several weeks
Before fading
Behind rich green
Elongated hearts
Of leafy green.

LILY OF THE VALLEY

Here comes summer, blooming and flourishing,
Furiously, gloriously greening uproariously.
Preening and posing , wanton and elegant.
Lustily, recklessly, fully, magnificent,
A season emergent with cross-pollination,
New shoots, new leaves, a new generation.
And there by the shed in the weeds of the alley
Lives the tiny pure lily, sweet maid of the valley.

LITTLE RED MEETS ROBIN RIDING

Robin and Little Red Riding Hood
Met one day, by chance, in the Forest Sherwood.
Rob was jogging along--not a thought in his head--
When he spied this sweet damsel all decked out in red.
She suddenly turned, and there Robin was,
Looking, well, looking--not like Santa Claus.

He wore fringes and felt, and a cap with a feather.
He carried his arrows in a long leather quiver.
"Well, hello, there," he called. "And who might you be?"
She squeaked out an "Eeek" and decided to flee.
Yes, she freaked when she saw him come riding that day
And, clutching her basket, she scurried away.

Then, urging his steed, over hillock, he sped,
Following the fleet-footed damsel in red.
Through Sherwood forest, and into the glen
Over the knoll, through the gorse in the fen,
Skirting the pond and up one more grade,
Then down an incline and into the glade.

But when he got to the rill of the brook
He stopped, reconnoitered. Where else could he look?
He crept up to the castle--just on a hunch
Where the Nottingham Sheriff was eating his lunch
He threw down his quiver and asked for some soup
Then gaffled some pie and ice-cream--one scoop.

I say Riding Hood should have taken a chance.
Old Robin just wanted a little romance.
But this fable of myth and legend and lore
Is making me yawn like never before.
You've all heard the stories.
That's it! There's no more!

LOVIN' MY LAPTOP

How I love my small computer
When I can easily reboot 'er.
And think of all the things I get
From surfing on the Internet.
Fingers dancing on the keys
Writing anything I please
Something bright something old
Sometimes dross and sometimes gold
All the grand thoughts, all the oldies
All the sayings, news or moldies.
In those bad old days of yore
When I typed my fingers sore
To get clean copy on the standard
Typewriter which demanded
Skill and care and close attention
To detail and intention.
Now I make my own mistakes
And then I do just what it takes
To fix the words to my approval
Or execute a quick removal.
Transposing letters is no problem.
My spell check will quickly solve them.
But now I see by this late hour
I must get out of bed and shower
And leave this toy for another day,
So I can go outside and play.
To pull my shoes on and some clothes
All set for town, whoever goes.

VALENTINE TO AN OCTOGENARIAN

Time's written lines on your dear face
That no cosmetic could erase.
But I still joy in your embrace,
My Valentine.

Though northern nights are long and cold
And sometimes dismal thoughts unfold,
Reminding us we're getting old.
Your hand's in mine.

Our bodies are wobbly, knobby, creaky
Uncertain, shaky, sometimes leaky,
Have acquired twinges that are sneaky.
But life's still fine.

And though it might be more desirable
To have a memory that's reliable.
There's one factor undeniable,
For you I pine.

No matter how you growl and mutter
You still make this old ticker flutter
(I did not say, "pass the butter.")
"Have more wine?"

We forfeit fashion for warming fleece
Wear slippers to give our feet some ease.
But we can still hug when we please….
Ah, that's divine!
To make you hear, I'd have to shout.
That's what these words are all about.
You may be old, but you're my boy scout,
My Valentine.

MINETTE

Let me tell you of Minette,
Robert's high-falutin' pet.
Snippy, arrogant and rude,
This puss has got an attitude.

Hostile, menacing and mean
She tears up the window screen.
And she's sure to exercise her will
When I try to make her take a pill.

If in a moment of wedded bliss
I move to give my mate a kiss
With claw unsheathed, she lashes out
And scratches me across the snout.

When she can't find the dog to bug
She'll sprawl akimbo on the rug
And lie in wait for another cat
That evil, sneaky, tricky brat.

If she's outside and I hear her whine
And I let her in for the umpteenth time.
She'll stay and nuzzle Robert's sweater
And purr until she's feeling better.

MULTITASKING

All day I've been
Tidying,
Puttering, muttering, sputtering,
Huffing, chuffing, puffing
Dipping, stripping, clipping, tripping
Over cats and dogs
And other sods.

And then I was
Shoveling,
Neatening, cleaning, gleaning,
Fussing, cussing,
Mopping, slopping, hopping,
Then, stopping
To cook lunch
For the whole bunch.

Afterwards there was
Swabbing,
Swishing, rinsing, wiping,
Sending, bending,
Toiling, boiling, foiling,
Shaking, baking, raking, flaking,
Wringing, washing, noshing, sloshing,
Sweeping,
And generally keeping
My house in order...
Sort 'er.

MY DOG JAKE

My dog Jake is a most handsome fellow
With a cold black nose, and a coat of yellow.
He's mischievous and lazy and lolls in the shade
The hair 'tween on his toes make his feet look frayed.

His manners are not the best, I'll agree.
He sticks his tongue out at people, you see.
He barks at the cars and teases the cat
He's a thief and scoundrel. I'll admit that.

Some hot cross buns, he once grabbed from the table
And got out the door before I was able
To catch him and cuff him and get back the plate.
Since once he had them, it was already too late.

He chews on tin cans and swims in the brook
He hangs around under foot when I cook.
Though he's always ready to ride in the truck.
He was no help at all, the time we got stuck.

And sometimes he doesn't smell all that sweet.
And he does not keep his house very neat.
He stays out in the rain and then gives great shake.
And showers the carpet, he does, dear old Jake.

But, he's my dog, and my friend and my golden cushion
And as for his manners, well, I am past pushin'
Him to behave like a dog should behave.
He's got me well trained--and I guess that's okay.

NEWS FROM THE BOONIES

Greetings dear friends. There's been little news.
We've somehow avoided the deep winter blues.
There's been no excitement, no tragic event.
So we're hibernating, relaxed and content,
Napping and chatting, ignoring the clock.
We've listened to music and taken our walk.
Made chili and cornbread, cheesecake and stew,
Played some gin rummy and stared at the view
Of the birds at the feeder, the squirrels in the pines,
The shimmering snow drifts, the ice on the lines.
We've heard the big ploughs, seen them salting roads
Heard the whine of the transports, bringing in loads
Of bananas and oranges and grapes from the South,
Tomatoes, and lemons that pucker your mouth.
We've filed income taxes, bought licenses, too.
Registered vehicles like good citizens do.
We've taken our vitamins, had our eyes tested.
Went to town shopping, came home and rested.
Now we sit in our armchairs and pity poor slobs
Who climb in cold cars and then rush off to jobs.
(There's nothing so pleasing as being retired
No cantankerous boss, no chance to get fired.)
Yes, we, with our toes up, are watching TV--
The O'Reilly Factor. Can't miss Jeopardy.
Looking forward to spring. We're counting our loonies.
Bye, bye for now. That's the news from the boonies.

OLD WOMAN ON THE BACK PORCH

There's work that I should do today
Instead I think I'd rather stay
And dream of times that used to be
When I was young and strong and free
Of pains and aches that build a cage
And keep one prisoner of age.

I'll ramble over grassy hills
Until my soul with sunlight fills
I'll walk in fields 'neath azure skies,
In clover, kissed by butterflies,
Or make wet footprints in the sand
A smooth round pebble in my hand.

I'll taste the spray upon my face.
Recall again a warm embrace.
I'll hear the songs we used to sing
And sip my coffee, savoring
Each memory of tenderness
The shape of every happiness.

I think I'll take an hour or two
To ponder of things we used to do
And why we went our separate ways
And wasted all those summer days,
Although we knew it couldn't last
The time, too soon, for us was past.

Still, there's today, and as I see
It, brim with possibility
And I can choose the way I fill it
Sad or happy, as I will it.
I think I'll find a shady nook
A gentle breeze, a favorite book.

ONCE I HAD

Once I had energy to burn
I challenged fate at every turn.
I did just as I pleased.
These days I find I tend to yearn
For folks who's company I spurned
and wish I had appeased.

Once I was hot and young and bold
But now I'm old and mind the cold
Especially on my back.
I really don't know what to do.
My hands and feet and nose turn blue,
My mood goes glum and black.

Would that time could flex and twist
And from one's shameful debit list
A wrong could be made right.
And happiness might now exist.
I'd overlook the things I missed
And easy sleep at night.

Sometimes I feel I've gone insane
In darkest hours, the terrors reign.
My life feels tipped askew.
I groan and weep and moan again
Naught's to be had to ease the pain
For all I can't undo.

But morning dawns and in the day
I see the clouds have blown away.
The ice begins to melt.
And so once more I choose to stay,
To face whatever comes my way.
And play the hand I'm dealt.

ONCE UPON A SUNDAY

Once upon a Sunday,
We watched the sun come up,
Drank a pot of coffee
And shared a dream or two.

Once upon a Sunday
We smelled a dying rose
Tasted golden fall
And marveled
For a bit.

Once upon a Sunday,
We laughed and ran,
Hung upside down
On the same tree limb,
Kicked the fallen leaves
And made a memory.

IS THIS SUNSHINE

Is this sunshine a truthful sign
Of welcome warm spring days sublime?
Beneath the soil, do tulips twirl
Do jaunty jonquils twist and whirl
As heat streams down and focuses
On lupine roots and crocuses,
Are worthy gardeners digging yet?
Should we be buying plants to set
Or should we wait a month or two
For shoots of green and skies of blue?
Do I sit back and plan some more
While kittens frolic on the floor?
Every year I wish and wonder,
Do I begin or wait and blunder?
Oh sure, I know it's much too soon.
Here in the swamp I start in June.

SPRING

It's spring, that season of the year
When ice and snow fast disappear.
When bards of poetry and rhyme
Set pen to paper one more time.

It's spring. The sap is on the rise.
The birds return to northern skies.
Small girls with high and lilting cries
New games with skipping ropes devise.

There's much to do while freshets run,
And new lambs frolic in the sun
And all young boys are having fun
With baseball glove and water gun.

The wife, who dust and dirt deplores,
Throws up the windows, opens doors
Shakes out the carpets, sweeps the floors.
Covers, cushions, drapes, restores.

Now scarves and boots and mitts must go
In boxes for eight months or so.
Pack up the woolens. Put on jeans.
Repaint the sashes. Frame the screens.

Put up the snowshoes and the skis.
Leave VCRs, board games, TVs.
Graft scions on young apple trees.
Put new wax in the hives for bees.

Plant garden, sow the flower bed.
Take out the trash and clean the shed.
Fix the fence and rake the lawn.
Spring's here at last, and winter's gone.

Find your straw hat, tip the brim.
Go to the river on a whim.
Take time to see the wild geese swim.
As the warm spring evening sky grows dim.

Spring is the season of new hope.
When snowdrifts leave the barren slope.
When new leaves bud on naked bush.
And chicks crack through their shells and push.
And hares from winter white turn brown
And ducks refresh their eiderdown.
And no one can recall a frown.
In either country or in town.
It's spring!

SUSAN PLAYS THE PIANO

Susan plays the piano.
Little trinkets of melody
Dappling the afternoon with gold,
Fingers touching joy bell,
Dancing,
Skipping,
Airy, light,
Cascading down the keys.

Susan plays the piano,
Knitting chords, spirit-like,
Swift,
Chased by thundering basses.
Low, now building,
Growing, swelling,
Full, flying,
Soaring to crescendo.

Then floating,
Echoing,
Splinters of crystal sound,
Flowing back
Quietly as breath.
A sighing.
Susan plays the piano
And I listen.

THE MISFIT

Unplanned, unwanted and unneeded,
Alone, despairing and unheeded.
Raised on pain and shame and guilt
Each skill and talent left to wilt
Taught to always know her place,
To serve in silence and with grace.

She never owned a Barbie doll
With golden hair and vapid stare.
Born out of step with age and group
She never spun a hula hoop.
She never had a poodle-skirt.
She never wore a body shirt.

She tried pin curls and penny loafers,
Plaids and pleats and peddle pushers.
She listened to the radio.
To Patsy, Kitty and Hank Snow.
With "Crazy Arms" she loved Ray Price.
She knew all nuances of "nice."

She never played a hand of Whist.
She never learned to do the twist.
In sports she never made the game.
In music she fared much the same.
Green and gauche and much too tall
Those golden years were not, at all.

SOME DAY YOU'LL BE MIDDLE AGED!

If I should tell you, on my oath,
What extraordinary feat is growth,
And that the measure of one's worth
Conforms to amplitude of girth;
That fortune frowns on natural teeth,
But glows upon the chins beneath,
I'd just be wasting precious breath.
You'd likely laugh yourself to death.
Alas, the nature of this truth
Is wholly lost on mocking youth.

THE THIEF

When he entered her home that night
And rummaged through her things
He found some cash, a bracelet,
A necklace and some rings.

Stuff that he could fence or pawn
Was all he cared about
As he rifled through the cupboards
And dumped the drawers all out.

But it wasn't just the things he took
Or the mess he left behind.
Much worse, that sly and heartless crook
Destroyed her peace of mind.

TRULY TIRED

I'm truly tired of all this snow,
Of mornings zero or below,
Of piling drifts and wind that lashes,
Freezing shut the window sashes,
Of damp and chills and frost and ice,
Of Scrabble games and cards and dice,
Of coughs and sneezes, pains and aches,
The stove and all the wood it takes,
Of mittens, parkas, boots and hats,
Oh whining dogs and shedding cats.

I need some green, a flower bud,
Some freshet water, even mud,
A pussy willow, a garden patch
A window raised, an open latch.
Where is that long awaited spring
Of which the birds and poets sing?
More weeks to wait? I want it now.
Away with snowshoes, skates and plough.

But, stop...it's wrong to mourn the day,
To gripe and wish my life away.
Yes, it's bad, but it could be worse.
In fact, it's sort of like this verse.

TO ROBERT ON OUR ANNIVERSARY

Sometimes you're a pussy cat.
And sometimes I'm a crab.
Quite often you're a fire ball.
At times I'm just drab.
Sometimes you're dense as fire wood.
I'm lucid as a stone.
You often want an audience.
I need to be alone.
You like to stay up late at night.
At nine I go to bed.
You like to hear disastrous news.
I'd rather hide my head.
I like to shop and talk with friends.
You're always in a rush.
You keep abreast of politics.
I scour out the flush.
We've been together seven years.
The days have rippled past.
Despite our faults and differences,
It's mostly been a blast.
And though we've had our ups and downs,
I know one thing that's true.
Of all the folks in all the world,
I'd rather be with you.

TODAY'S ALL THAT MATTERS

When I hear someone talk of the "good old days"
Their memories glowing through time's purple haze,
I admire their joy as they pick through the past,
Insisting their childhood was one great big blast.

My youth swirled in anger, anxiety and guilt
That smothered my spirit like a damp mildewed quilt.
Forever admonished to behave like my cousin
Who was pretty and sweet, and wore smiles by the dozen.

Like a wild thing on Dexedrine I chomped at the bit
If there ever was trouble on the hoof, I was it.
I hated to conform, to submit, to comply.
When the boys gave me trouble, why, I blacked their eye.

My mother despaired of my bad attitude
Of my turbulent nature, my manner so crude:
"Be, nice, be quiet, be a lady, be still.
Don't climb like a tomboy, don't stram down the hill.

"Stop what you're doing, and go get the eggs.
Quit picking the scabs off your elbows and legs.
Don't race with the boys. Don't wrestle. Don't twirl,
Now clean off the table. Sit down. You're a girl.

"Wash the cream separator, sweep the porch with the broom.
Make your tangled hair tidy. Go clean up your room.
Watch your language, young lady. And, no talking back.
You'll be sent to reform school, and that will be that."

"Ah, Willie, they mourned..."if she'd followed the rules,
Why she had the brains, the skills and the tools,
To be something bigger, something extr'ordinary,
Like an Eastern Star Member, or a top secretary."

No. I was a brat, a snarler, a fighter,
Who wound up a yarn-spinner wordsmith and writer.
I never did anything the way I was told.
I just spend each new day as if it was gold.

So the past can stay buried. It's ashes and rust.
Yesterday's nothing but illusion and dust.
Today's all that matters, just these golden hours,
With friends, lover, family, my critters and flowers.

SUMMER HEAT

If summer heat has got you beat
And left you drenched and panting
If humid days and muggy nights
Are setting you to ranting.

Think about six months from now
When every day it's snowing,
And you're in ski-suits, boots and mitts
'Cause bitter winds are blowing.

And it's so cold your car won't start
The heater's blocked with ice,
And school is cancelled once again,
Now, isn't summer nice?

WE NEED TREES

For totems and paddles and spear shafts and bows,
For snowshoes and baskets and handles for hoes,
For fibres and fuels and clothing and twine,
For tanning the leather and making our wine,
For matting and planking and fine cedar chests,
For toys and whistles and dyeing our vests,
For boxes and buckets and beehives and bats,
For cardboard and coffins and cheese crates and vats,
For dressers and sideboards and breadboards and masks,
For rockers and fence posts and counters and casks,
For picture frames, tables, toboggans and sleds,
For dog houses, lattices, cow barns and sheds,
For cradles and ladles and wooden high chairs,
For banisters, step stools and swing seats and stairs.
For roofing and rafters and shingles and doors,
For braces and studding and ceilings and floors,
For ladders and lodge poles and sailing boat masts,
For sign posts and billboards, rail fences that last.
Scrabble tiles, abacus, handrails and harps
For checkers and teeters for kids in the parks
For desks and credenzas, cellos and flutes
For big grand pianos and fiddles and lutes
For churches and cabins, steeples and piers
For bridges and benches that last through the years.
For pickets and placards, and corn cribs and crutches
For butcher blocks, cabinets, cupboards and hutches,
For carving boards, flour bins, hat racks and ramps
For boardwalks and shelves for collectors of stamps.
For potato barrels, for skis and for canes
For shelters that keep our things dry when it rains.
For turpentine, resin, for newsprint and pews
For syrups, elixirs and heels in our shoes.
So many things come--for you and for me--
From the root, wood, bark, berries and leaves of a tree.
Plant a tree.

VALENTINE'S DAY

Here's to all sweethearts
Who never grow old,
With a love that lives daily
As precious as gold.
To September lovers
To weddings in June;
To romance in the garden
By the light of the moon.
To loves unrequited,
To love that has been.
To love once gone sour,
Turned sweet once again.
To romantics and poets
And young lovers naive,
To the sensitive one
With his heart on his sleeve.
To love that is won
And to love that is lost,
To love's wild abandon
Discounting the cost.
Here's to the sad loves
The ones who know better
But who shed salty tears
On a faded love letter.
To love that is faithful
To love that is true.
To those who write odes
To eyes green, brown and blue.
To puppy love, wistful
With wonder, insane.
Full of strange giddy feelings
And sorrow and pain.
To lovers long married
Who are still holding hands
True to vows old and strong
As their worn wedding bands.

To those everywhere
Who have felt Cupid's dart,
When one unique being
Has captured their heart.
They find by a smile,
Voice or figure, they're smitten,
And their feet begin dancing
When the love bug has bitten.
To lovers world over,
Here's to you, I say.
Have a wonderful, lovingful
Valentine's day.

SLEEPLESS IN WILMOT

For us moldy oldies, nights are long,
Restive, wide-eyed waits for the dawn.
As digital clocks flash hourly numbers
I envy youth their peaceful slumbers.

To fill the dark and silent hours,
I count the species of wild flowers
That bloom unbidden in my field,
Give thanks for the potato yield.

Or contemplate the falling snow
Swirling, soft in the yard light's glow.
I hear the dog moan in her dreams
And wonder at the kitten's schemes.

I mourn lost friends in lonely sorrow.
I plan what I should wear tomorrow.
I wonder how I got these wrinkles,
Why grins surround the eyes in crinkles.

When do I rest? Ah, there's the rub.
I sleep quite soundly in the tub.
And I can always sleep in church
And snore and gape and drool and lurch.

Sometimes while reading, eyelids droop.
I've been caught nodding at my soup.
And no amount of clever tricks
Jolt me to ponder politics.

It doesn't help a lot I've found
To lie in bed and toss around.
The best cure I've discovered yet
Is switching on the Internet.

Knowing there're others just like me,
Out there, wide-eyed, and brewing tea.
(Why, they may be doing something worse,
Than typing, tapping lines of verse.)

They, too, count money and woolly sheep.
Some even cook or dust or sweep.
They listen to the stomach rumbles
And deeper sleepers' lowing mumbles.

They swing upright, toss back the sheet
And search for slippers with their feet.
Knowing when they're feeling cold,
That's just the cost of getting old.

So I'm no different from other older folks
Who pace the nights in fleecy cloaks.
They also make the bathroom run
While they await tomorrow's sun.

WHEN ELEPHANTS SPIN TAFETA

A headache thrummed across my brow.
My bones were feeling achy.
I took some capsuled Tylenol,
As I was feeling shaky.

Then I ate a stalk of celery
Before I went to bed,
Which caused a big hilarity
To rattle in my head.

I saw elephants spin taffeta
And crocodiles tat lace,
Then I pinned gophers to my hair
To polka dot my face.

I tied a moonbeam on a string
And wrapped it round a tree
Then took a waffle from a trunk
So it would play with me.

The panda bears wore rosaries
The wolves step out with pigs
I tapped the fiddle headed sticks
And wrapped my nose with twigs.

It made a caterpillar smile,
To use a toad for strings
While dandelions smiled aloud
At purple musk ox wings.

I took a nightmare dancing.
We did the bug-a-lug.
As all the snails were prancing
Around a Toby jug.

Then starlight sparkled in my soup.
My bed flew in the air.
My toes all twinkled in their socks,
Across the thoroughfare.

And then I saw butterfly
Make fudge with nuts in it.
And a porcupine that closed its eyes
And sang the alphabet.

You'd have a small idea of
The things that made me laugh.
Why an armadillo blew his nose
And ate a paragraph.

Then morning came and I awoke
And stretched this way and that.
But imagine my astonishment
When I saw the dog and cat!

They all had diamonds in their ears,
Wore taffeta and lace.
Their tails were tied in granny knots
When they sailed off in space.

The porridge bowl was made of fur,
And snow-flakes all were round
And full moons e-mailed meteors
With quadraphonic sound.

I wondered what would happen next
And just what I should do.
I coughed and blew my nose and sneezed.
Alas, I had the flu.

WRITE TIME

The house has gone quiet,
The critters are calm,
Our guests have returned
To the place they are from.
My man's in his chair,
At peace, fast asleep,
The moment has come
Which allows me to keep,
That same old promise
I've been making forever:
To sit down and write.
Yes, it's now or never.
I will pen the profound,
The clever, the droll,
And keep words coming
Now I'm on a roll.
My soul and my spirit
Are aflame with desire,
To speak, to be heard,
To make use of my power.
To transcend the mundane
To awaken the mind
To leave the dreary,
The dull, far behind.
But before I can soar
To the heavens or higher
I'll just stop once more
To put clothes in the dryer.
I'll refill the washer
And sort out a load
Of towels and bedding.
Uh Oh! Yes I know
Where this is heading.
Yesterday's thoughts
Which I wanted to capture,
Were so fit, so right on,
They filled me with rapture.

Now I stare at white space.
What sounded so right
As it whirled through my head
Must have died in the night.
Those fine words have vanished.
(I delete and erase.)
The muse is unyielding.
My memory, like Elvis,
Has now left the building.

WRITER'S LAMENT

Snow falls, time crawls, the man calls.
I've sprawled, scrawled, scrolled, trolled
Rolled through the pages, for ages, fingering, malingering,
Searching for spots of thoughts and droll whatnots,
To no avail.
I wail and rail and flail at words grown stale.
I long for some vim, some valour and colour, not dolour, not duller,
Not dreary and weary and teary and smeary
But bright and sharp like fins on a carp
All glittering, twittering, alittering, flittering
Over planks of shanks, like blanks on bridges
With clefts and ridges, arches and bumps
Instead I pull puling phrases in lumps.
I'm sitting, effacing, disgracing, erasing the spaces,
Drawing new faces in places where words fall short.
No longer intrepid, just vapid, insipid.
Not lively and lucid but stilted and stupid.
Word-weak and wallowing, following, swallowing
Tired old tripe, neither rare nor ripe.
So, sighing with chagrin, contrition and shame
With nothing or no one or no where to blame,
I'll go into the house and cover my sorrow,
And wait for my muse to come calling tomorrow.

HAS THERE EVER BEEN A SKY SO BLUE?

Has there ever been a sky so blue
A color of such an awesome hue
That reaches into the furthest yonder?
The touch of cobalt makes me ponder
The shades of the ever-changing sky.
Cerulean when no haze is nigh.
Azure, it seems, then I gaze higher
A sun-blissed bowl of rich sapphire.

But, oh, it's apple blossom time!
The heady scent is so sublime
I close my eyes, inhaling deep
The awesome joy I like to keep
Safe and sure within my heart.
When petals, pink and white, depart.
In times when only dark clouds roll
Their gentle glory will heal my soul.